I CAN MAKE IT!
I CAN READ IT!

20 Reproducible Booklets to Develop Early Literacy Skills

WINTER

WRITTEN BY:

Nancy Anderson, Linda Morgason, Jan Robbins

EDITED BY:

Mary Lester

Kim T. Griswell

ILLUSTRATED BY:

Mary Lester

COVER DESIGN BY:

Nick Greenwood and Kimberly Richard

www.themailbox.com

©2000 by THE EDUCATION CENTER, INC.
All rights reserved.

ISBN# 1-56234-398-X

Manufactured in the United States
10 9 8 7 6 5 4 3 2

TABLE OF CONTENTS

HELLO, SUN! GOOD NIGHT, MOON!

Brighten your students' day with this interactive booklet about the sun and moon! Give each student a brad and a copy of pages 4–7. Instruct the student to color and then cut out her booklet pages and disc. Have her insert her brad through the circle on booklet page 6 and then through the circle on the disc. Next, direct her to stack the pages in numerical order, placing the cover on top. Staple the pages on the left-hand side, making sure the disc is not stapled. Then read the completed booklet while students follow along. Demonstrate how to rotate the disc to reveal the appropriate illustration for each page. Provide time for each student to read her booklet with a buddy. Then encourage her to take her booklet home to read to family members. Day in and day out, reading to parents is the thing to do!

CREATIVE DECORATING OPTIONS

- On the disc, add glitter to the sun's rays.
- On the disc, add star stickers around the moon.

Extend this booklet activity by reading aloud *Brown Cow, Green Grass, Yellow Mellow Sun* by Ellen Jackson (Disney Press, 1997) and *Papa, Please Get the Moon for Me* by Eric Carle (Simon & Schuster Children's Division, 1991).

3

Booklet Page and Cover

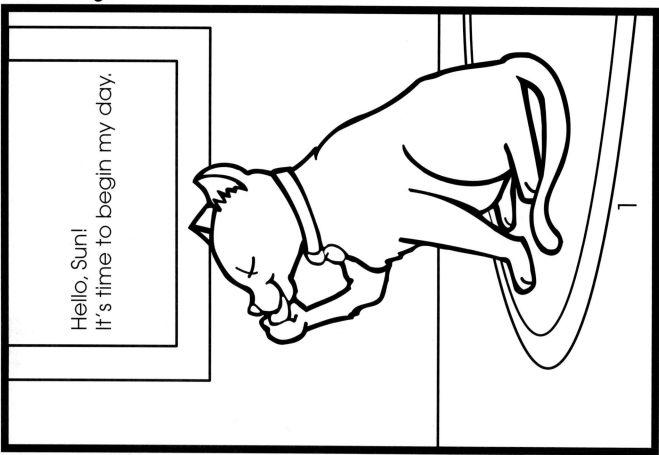

Hello, Sun!
It's time to begin my day.

1

Cover

Hello, Sun!
Good Night, Moon!

Name _____

©2000 The Education Center, Inc.

Note to the teacher: Use with "Hello, Sun! Good Night, Moon!" on page 3.

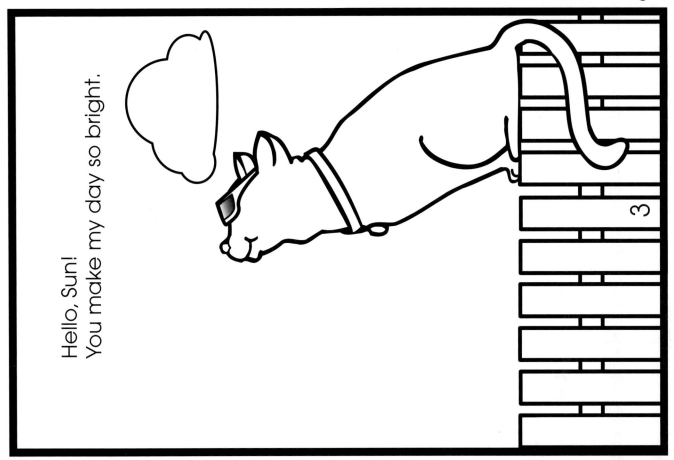

Hello, Sun!
You make my day so bright.

3

Good night, Moon!
It's time to end my play.

2

Hello, Sun!
You help the plants grow.

5

Good night, Moon!
You shine on me at night.

4

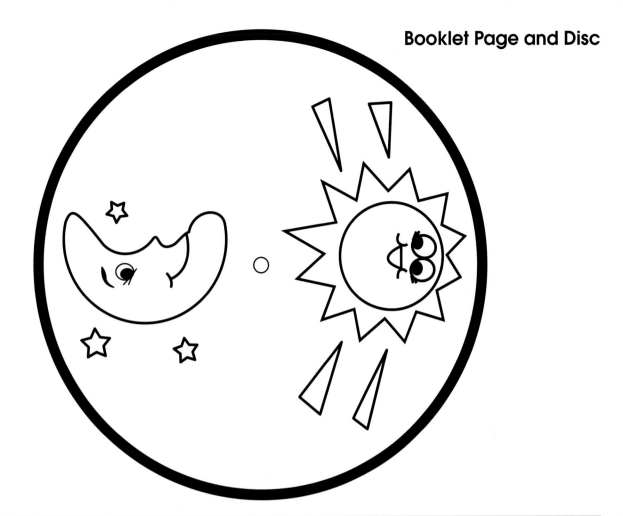

Good night, Moon.
It's time to go to sleep, I know...

So tomorrow I can say,
"Hello, Sun!
Good night, Moon!"

6

Note to the teacher: Use with "Hello, Sun! Good Night, Moon!" on page 3.

TICK, TOCK! TICK, TOCK!

Add a new twist to reading and telling time with this hands-on interactive booklet! Give each student a brad, a copy of pages 10 and 11, and a construction paper copy of page 9. Read with students pages 10 and 11, directing them to write a time on the appropriate lines. Then have each student color and cut out the booklet pages and patterns. Have him stack his pages in order and staple them to the clock where indicated. Next, help him punch holes in the clock hands, align the holes with the clock's center circle, and insert the brad. Demonstrate how to read the booklet by reading a page and setting the clock hands to correspond with the text. Provide time for each student to read his booklet with a buddy before sending it home to read to family members. What a timely booklet for reading!

CREATIVE DECORATING OPTIONS

- Use puffy paint to outline the numerals on the clock.
- Tie a piece of yarn to a jingle bell. Staple the yarn to the back of the clock behind the booklet pages. As students read that it is time to get up, encourage them to shake their booklets to make the "alarm" ring.

Tick, Tock! Tick, Tock!

_____ Mike _____'s clock

To extend this booklet activity, make a class book of students' favorite times of day. Have each student write about and illustrate his favorite time of day. Invite each student to read his response to the class and set his booklet clock to the corresponding time. Then stack the students' papers between two sheets of construction paper and staple the sides. Title the book "The BEST Time of Day!"

Booklet Patterns

Clock Hands

Clock

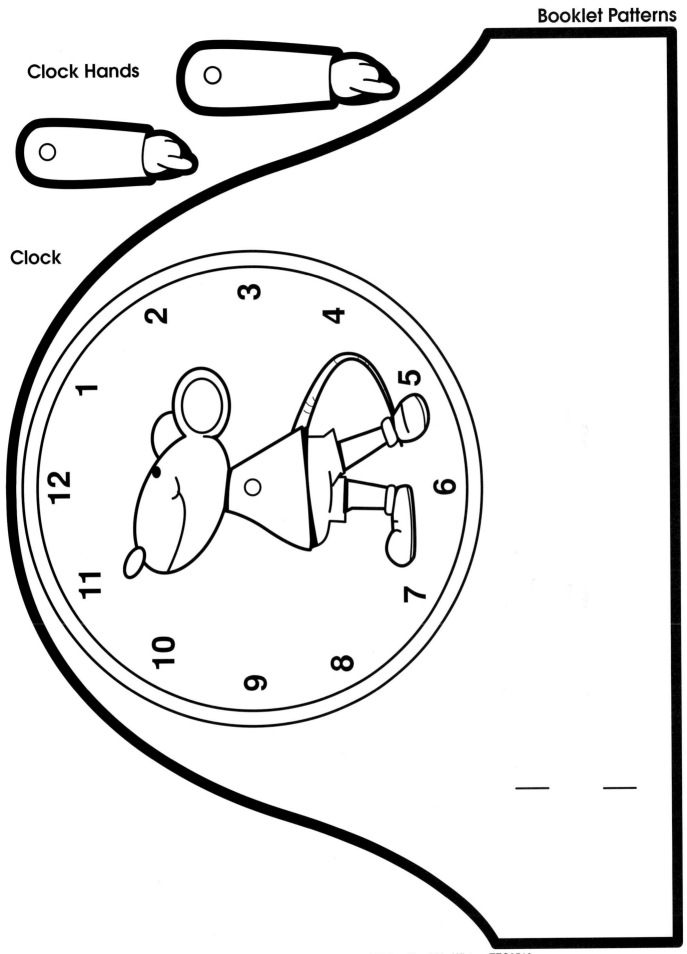

Note to the teacher: Use with "Tick, Tock! Tick, Tock!" on page 8.

Booklet Cover and Pages
Cover

Tick, Tock! Tick, Tock!

_____ 's clock

Pages

"Tick, tock," says the clock.
"It's time to get up.

It's _____ o'clock."

1

"Tick, tock," says the clock.
"It's time to go to school.

It's _____ o'clock."

2

"Tick, tock," says the clock.
"It's time to eat lunch.

It's _____ o'clock."

3

"Tick, tock," says the clock.
"It's time to ride the bus home.

It's _____ o'clock."

4

Note to the teacher: Use with "Tick, Tock! Tick, Tock!" on page 8.

"Tick, tock," says the clock.
"It's time to play with friends.

It's _____ o'clock."

5

"Tick, tock," says the clock.
"It's time to eat dinner.

It's _____ o'clock."

6

"Tick, tock," says the clock.
"It's time to take a bath.

It's _____ o'clock."

7

"Tick, tock," says the clock.
"It's time to go to bed.

It's _____ o'clock."

8

"Good night," says the clock.
"It's time to go to sleep!"

9

Note to the teacher: Use with "Tick, Tock! Tick, Tock!" on page 8.

THE HONEY PARTY

Here's an adorable rhyming booklet that your youngsters can't bear to be without! Give each student a copy of pages 14–15 and a brown construction paper copy of page 13. Read pages 14 and 15 with students. Then have each student color the booklet pages. (Remind students to color lightly over the text so that the story can be read.) Next, direct the student to cut out the pattern and booklet pages on the bold outer lines. Have her stack her pages in numerical order, placing the cover on top. Instruct her to staple the booklet pages to the bear's shoulders as illustrated. Provide time for students to read their completed booklets with one another. Then encourage students to take their booklets home to read to family members. Parents will enjoy hearing this honey of a booklet!

CREATIVE DECORATING OPTIONS

- Tie a colorful ribbon around the bear's neck.
- Glue a button at the center of the cover's neckline.

The Honey Party

Rachelle
Name

Extend the teddy bear theme by using Teddy Grahams® crackers as math counters.

HONEY

Note to the teacher: Use with "The Honey Party" on page 12.

Booklet Page and Cover

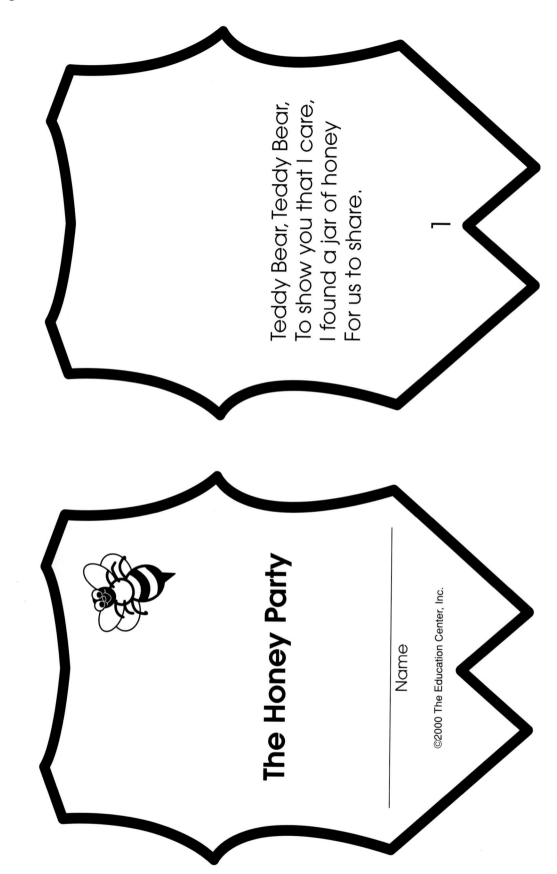

Teddy Bear, Teddy Bear,
To show you that I care,
I found a jar of honey
For us to share.

1

Cover

The Honey Party

Name _____

©2000 The Education Center, Inc.

©2000 The Education Center, Inc. • *I Can Make It! I Can Read It!* • *Winter* • TEC3510

14 **Note to the teacher:** Use with "The Honey Party" on page 12.

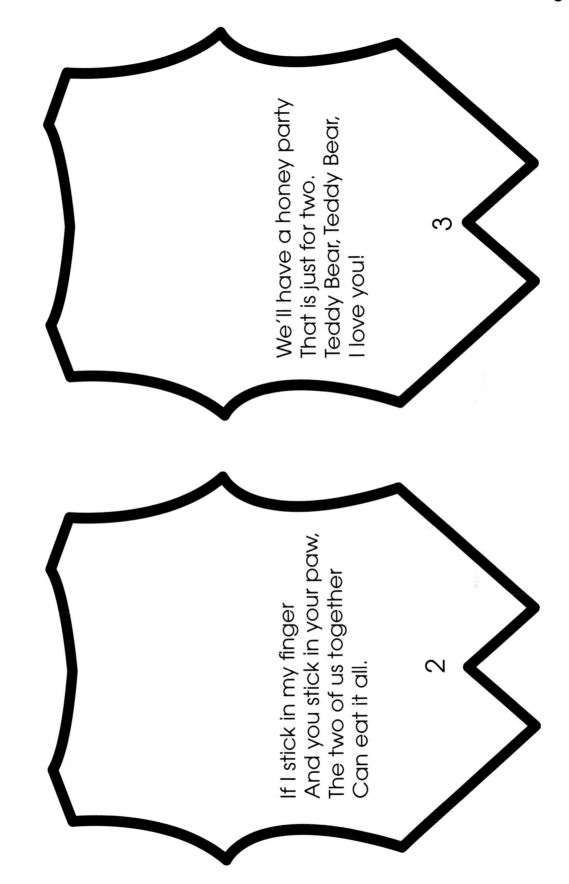

We'll have a honey party
That is just for two.
Teddy Bear, Teddy Bear,
I love you!

3

If I stick in my finger
And you stick in your paw,
The two of us together
Can eat it all.

2

Note to the teacher: Use with "The Honey Party" on page 12.

WHO IS MAKING THAT NOISE?

Treat your youngsters to a scrumptious round of reading with this predictable gingerbread boy booklet! Give each student a copy of pages 17–20. Instruct the student to cut out her cover, booklet pages, and patterns. Invite her to color booklet pages 1–6. Next, have her draw and color a design on each pattern and then glue each pattern on the corresponding page where indicated. Have her cut open the door flap on page 5. Then invite her to color and decorate her cover with art materials, such as yarn, puffy paint, and buttons. To assemble her booklet, instruct the student to stack her pages in numerical order, placing the cover on top. Have her staple the pages together as shown. Then read with students a completed booklet, lifting the flaps on each page as you read. Provide time for students to read their booklets with partners. Encourage students to take their booklets home to read to family members. Parents are sure to enjoy this sweet reading opportunity!

CREATIVE DECORATING OPTIONS

- Use the patterns as templates to cut out a table-cloth, a blanket, and a shower curtain from colorful wrapping papers.
- Lift each flap in the booklet and draw a picture of what Gingerbread Boy might find there.

To extend this booklet activity, read aloud Paul Galdone's *The Gingerbread Boy* (Clarion Books, 1983). Then serve your youngsters cold milk and crisp ginger cookies.

Gingerbread Boy ran to the k
Scritch, scratch, nibble!
"Who is making that noise?
He looked under the table.
No one was under the tabl

GLUE

Who Is Making That Noise?

Rasheeda
Name

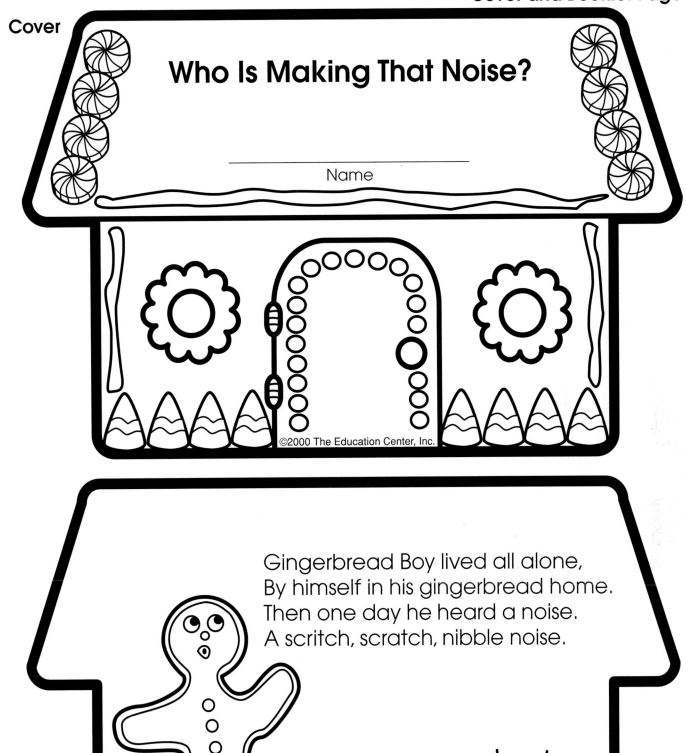

Who Is Making That Noise?

_____
Name

©2000 The Education Center, Inc.

Gingerbread Boy lived all alone,
By himself in his gingerbread home.
Then one day he heard a noise.
A scritch, scratch, nibble noise.

Scritch!
Scratch!
Nibble!

1

Gingerbread Boy ran to the kitchen.
Scritch, scratch, nibble!
"Who is making that noise?" he asked.
He looked under the table.
No one was under the table.

Glue.

2

He ran to the bedroom.
Scritch, scratch, nibble!
"Who is making that noise?" he asked.
He looked under the bed.
No one was under the bed.

Glue.

3

He ran to the bathroom.
Scritch, scratch, nibble!
"Who is making that noise?" he asked.
He looked in the tub.
No one was in the tub.

Glue.

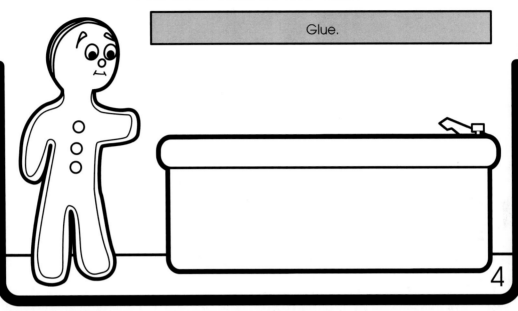

4

Gingerbread Boy ran to the front door.
Scritch, scratch, nibble!
"Who is making that noise?" he asked.
He opened the door.
Gingerbread Mouse was at his front door!

5

Note to the teacher: Use with "Who Is Making That Noise?" on page 16.

Booklet Page and Patterns

So Gingerbread Boy invited him in,
And pretty soon they were best friends.
Now Gingerbread Boy and Gingerbread Mouse
Live together in their gingerbread house.

6

Shower Curtain

Fold back. Glue to page 4.

Tablecloth

Fold back. Glue to page 2.

Blanket

Fold back. Glue to page 3.

©2000 The Education Center, Inc. • *I Can Make It! I Can Read It!* • Winter • TEC3510

20   **Note to the teacher:** Use with "Who Is Making That Noise?" on page 16.

I'M READY FOR HANUKKAH!

Here's a Hanukkah booklet that will put a new spin on your reading program! Give each student a copy of pages 23–24 and two copies of page 22. Have the student color the illustrations on the booklet pages. Then direct her to cut out the dreidel patterns and booklet pages on the bold outer lines. Next, instruct her to place her two dreidels on top of each other and then fold them on the dotted lines. Staple the dreidels together along the dotted lines, once each at the top and bottom. Direct the student to stack her booklet pages in numerical order. Then instruct her to glue booklet page 1 onto a page of the dreidel. Keeping her booklet pages in numerical order, have her glue the appropriate booklet page to each subsequent dreidel page. When students have completed their booklets, read one with students. Demonstrate how the dreidel is formed as the pages are read (see the illustration). Tell students that a dreidel is the top used to play the Hanukkah game mentioned on booklet page 5. Then provide time for each student to read her booklet to a buddy before taking it home to read to family members.

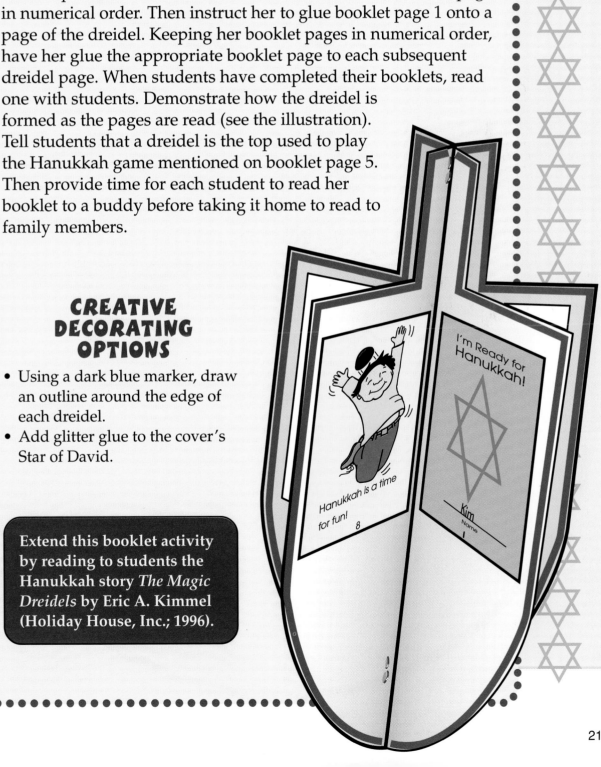

CREATIVE DECORATING OPTIONS

- Using a dark blue marker, draw an outline around the edge of each dreidel.
- Add glitter glue to the cover's Star of David.

Extend this booklet activity by reading to students the Hanukkah story *The Magic Dreidels* by Eric A. Kimmel (Holiday House, Inc.; 1996).

Booklet Pattern

Dreidel

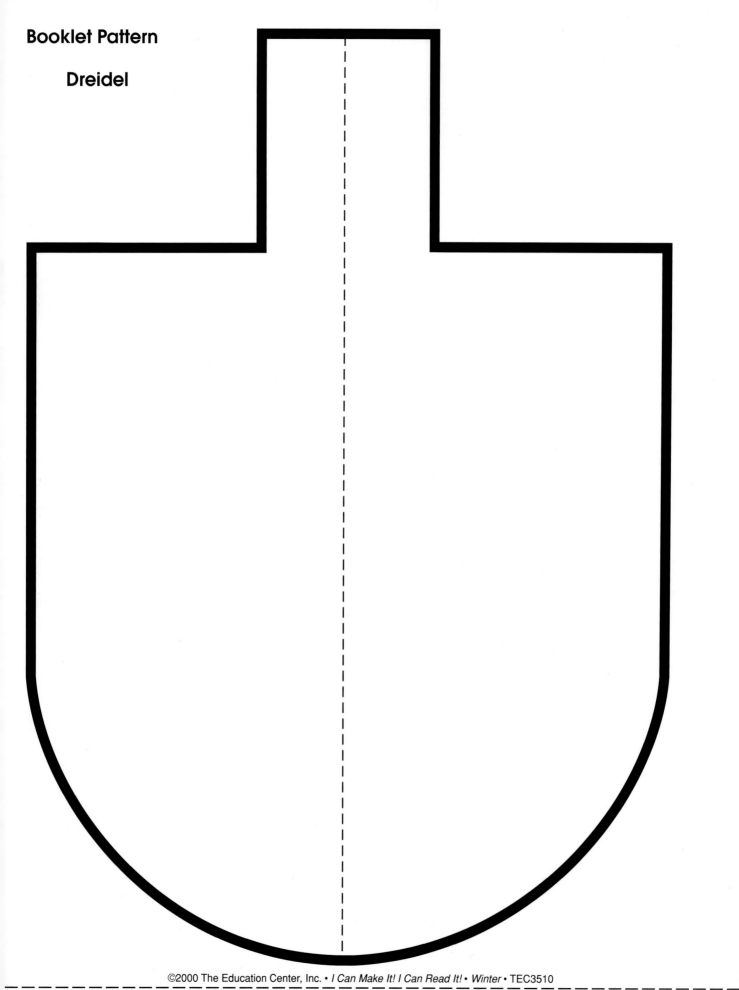

Note to the teacher: Use with "I'm Ready for Hanukkah!" on page 21.

I'm Ready for Hanukkah!

_____

Name

1

Hanukkah takes place in the winter. Hanukkah lasts eight days.

2

Hanukkah is a time to light candles.

3

Hanukkah is a time for giving presents.

4

Booklet Pages

Hanukkah is a time to play a fun game.

5

Hanukkah is a time to eat potato pancakes.

6

Hanukkah is a time for chocolate.

7

Hanukkah is a time for fun!

8

©2000 The Education Center, Inc. • *I Can Make It! I Can Read It!* • *Winter* • TEC3510

24 **Note to the teacher:** Use with "I'm Ready for Hanukkah!" on page 21.

A CHRISTMAS DREAM

Stuffing stockings has never been more fun than with this jolly rhyming booklet! Give each student a copy of pages 28–30, a red construction paper copy of page 26, and a white construction paper copy of page 27. Have each student color her booklet cover and stocking stuffers. Then instruct her to cut out the patterns and booklet pages on the bold lines. Next, direct her to glue the stocking top to the stocking where indicated and set it aside to dry. To assemble her booklet, the student stacks her booklet pages in numerical order, places them inside the folded booklet cover, and staples the left-hand side as illustrated. Finally, have her glue her booklet to her stocking. When the booklets have been completed, have students place their stockings and stocking stuffers on their desks. Then read the booklet with students, having each student place her appropriate card in the stocking when its matching text has been read. Provide time for her to practice reading with a friend. Encourage students to take their booklets home to read to family members and friends. Reading this booklet will make for a cool Yule!

CREATIVE DECORATING OPTIONS

- Glue cotton balls to the stocking top.
- Punch a hole in the top left-hand corner of the stocking. Tie a length of Christmas ribbon through the hole and hang the stockings on a bulletin board.

To extend this activity, direct each student to cut out magazine pictures of items that she would like to give to her family members. For each item, have her write a sentence that tells who would receive it and why. Then provide time for students to share their choices with the class.

A Christmas Dream

Sheena
Name

Booklet Pattern

Stocking

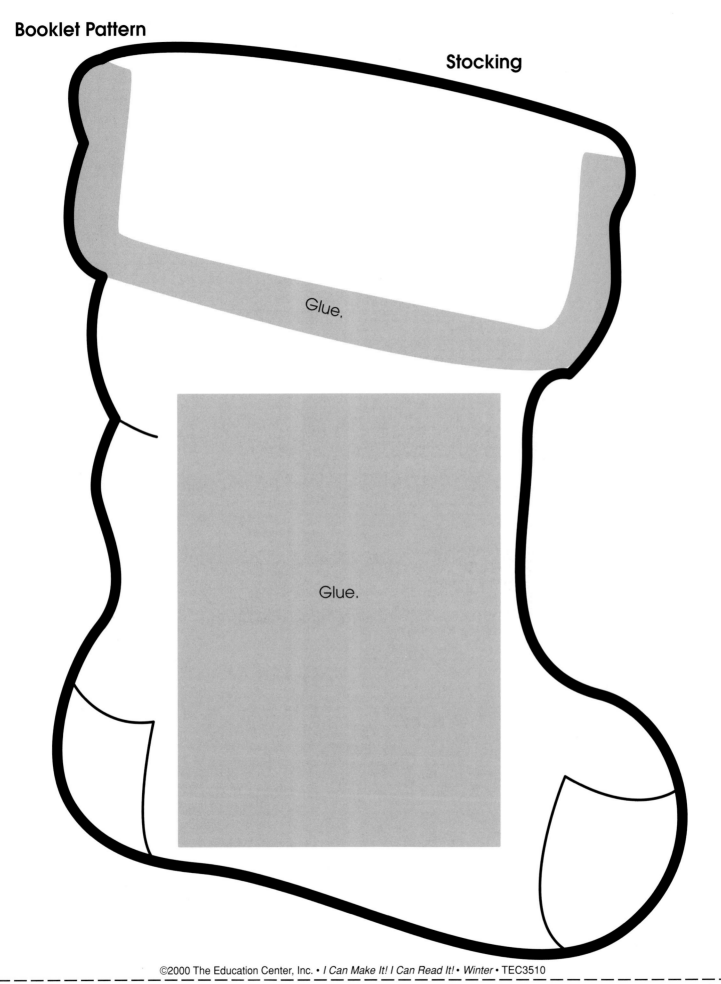

Glue.

Glue.

Note to the teacher: Use with "A Christmas Dream" on page 25.

Stocking Top

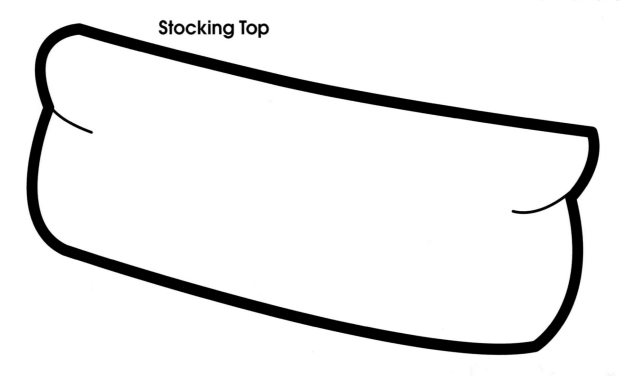

Booklet Cover

A
Christmas
Dream

_____
Name
©2000 The Education Center, Inc.

Note to the teacher: Use with "A Christmas Dream" on page 25.

When I dream of Christmas, what do I see?

I see presents for my family.

1

I see a Christmas cake for Uncle Frank, a laughing doll for Holly.

2

I see a big blue ball for baby Sam. Wouldn't that be jolly?

3

I see a yellow duck for brother Chuck, a drum for little Billy.

4

I see a bright red kite for cousin Jane and a jack-in-the-box. How silly!

5

I see stockings hung by the fire so bright.

6

I see children tucked in their beds tonight.

7

When I dream of Christmas, what do I see?

I see presents for my family.

8

Note to the teacher: Use with "A Christmas Dream" on page 25.

Stocking Stuffer Patterns

Christmas Cake

Jack-in-the-Box

Drum

Kite

Doll

Ball

Duck

Note to the teacher: Use with "A Christmas Dream" on page 25.

THE SEVEN DAYS OF KWANZAA

Students will strengthen reading skills *and* learn about a joyous African-American holiday with this Kwanzaa booklet. Give each student a copy of pages 32–34. Have the student color her booklet pattern and pages. (Remind her to color lightly over the text so the booklet can be read.) Then instruct her to cut out the pattern and pages on the bold outer lines. To assemble the booklet pages, direct the student to stack them in numerical order, placing the cover on top. Next, have her align the stack on top of Day 7 as shown and staple the pages at the left-hand side of the booklet. Read a completed booklet with students. Then provide time for each student to read her booklet with a partner. Then send the booklets home to be shared with family members. Parents will light up listening to their children read this informative booklet!

CREATIVE DECORATING OPTIONS

- Outline the flames with puffy paint.
- Use glitter glue on the flames.

To extend this booklet activity, read to students Andrea Davis Pinkney's *Seven Candles for Kwanzaa* (Dial Books for Young Readers, 1993).

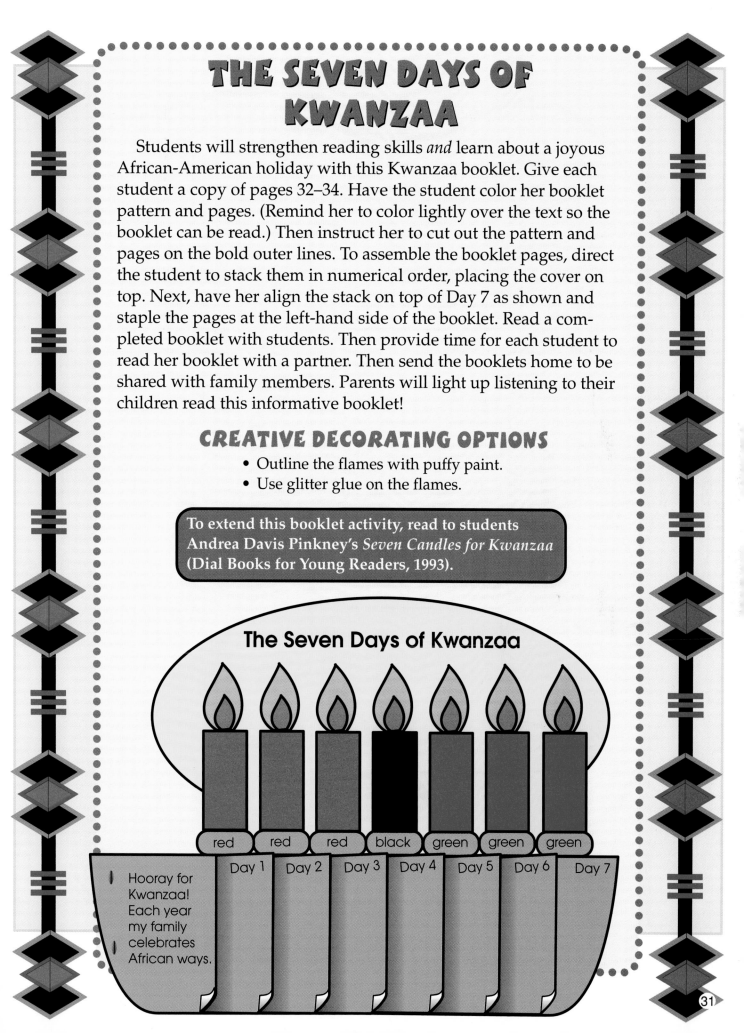

The Seven Days of Kwanzaa

red red red black green green green

Day 1   Day 2   Day 3   Day 4   Day 5   Day 6   Day 7

Hooray for Kwanzaa! Each year my family celebrates African ways.

Booklet Pattern

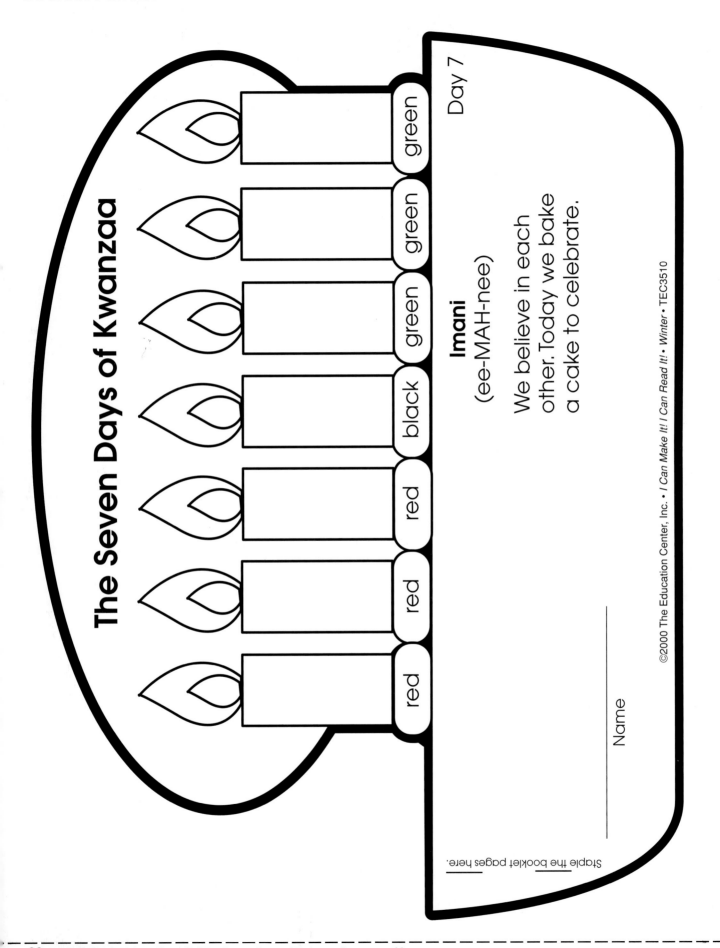

The Seven Days of Kwanzaa

green
green
green
black
red
red
red

Day 7

Imani
(ee-MAH-nee)

We believe in each other. Today we bake a cake to celebrate.

Name _____

Staple the booklet pages here.

Ujamma
(oo-jah-MAH)

Day 4

We help friends and neighbors. Today we plant trees in our city park.

Ujima
(oo-JEE-mah)

Day 3

We work together to make life better. Today we clean the house together.

Kujichagulia
(koo-jee-cha-goo-LEE-ah)

Day 2

We think for ourselves. Today we read a book about an African family.

Umoja
(oo-MO-jah)

Day 1

Everyone in my family works together. Today we cook together.

Note to the teacher: Use with "The Seven Days of Kwanzaa" on page 31.

Booklet Pages and Cover

Day 6

Kuumba
(koo-OOM-bah)

We make things. Today I sing a song I made up.

Day 5

Nia
(NEE-ah)

We talk about the future. Today I decide I will grow up to be a firefighter.

Cover

Hooray for Kwanzaa! Each year my family celebrates African ways.

©2000 The Education Center, Inc. • *I Can Make It! I Can Read It!* • *Winter* • TEC3510

34   **Note to the teacher:** Use with "The Seven Days of Kwanzaa" on page 31.

HIP! HOP! HAPPY NEW YEAR!

Reading confidence will grow in leaps and bounds with this New Year's bunny booklet! Give each student a copy of pages 37–39 and a white construction paper copy of page 36. Have the student color her booklet pages. (Remind her to color lightly over the text so the booklet can be read.) Then instruct her to cut out the booklet pages on the bold outer lines. Next, direct her to stack her pages in numerical order, placing the cover on top. Have her align her stacked pages with the hat on page 9 and then staple the booklet at the top. Read the booklet with students, assisting them with writing an answer on page 9. Then provide time for each student to practice reading her booklet with a partner. Encourage students to take their booklets home to read to family members and friends. Parents will be all ears!

Hip! Hop!
Happy New Year!

Michelle
Name

CREATIVE DECORATING OPTIONS

- Glue bingo markers to the cover.
- Glue a pom-pom or staple curling ribbon to the point of the booklet hat.

Extend this booklet activity by reading aloud *P. Bear's New Year's Party: A Counting Book* by Paul Owen Lewis (Tricycle Press, 1999).

Booklet Page

9

Note to the teacher: Use with "Hip! Hop! Happy New Year!" on page 35.

Cover

Hip! Hop!
Happy New Year!

Name

©2000 The Education Center, Inc.

For a hip, hop, happy
New Year's Day,

1

Hop over to a party and
get ready to play.

2

©2000 The Education Center, Inc. • *I Can Make It! I Can Read It!* • *Winter* • TEC3510

Booklet Pages

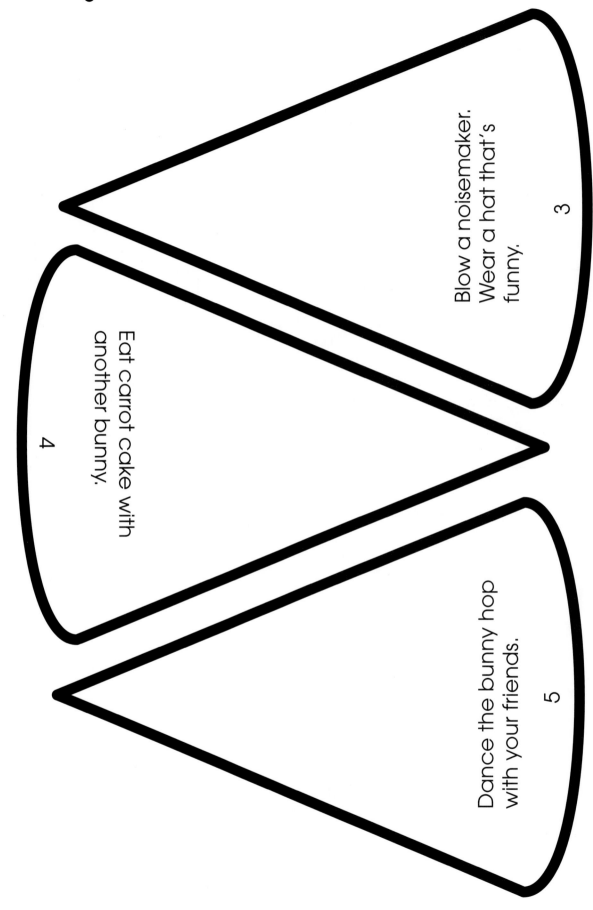

Blow a noisemaker.
Wear a hat that's
funny.

3

Eat carrot cake with
another bunny.

4

Dance the bunny hop
with your friends.

5

Note to the teacher: Use with "Hip! Hop! Happy New Year!" on page 35.

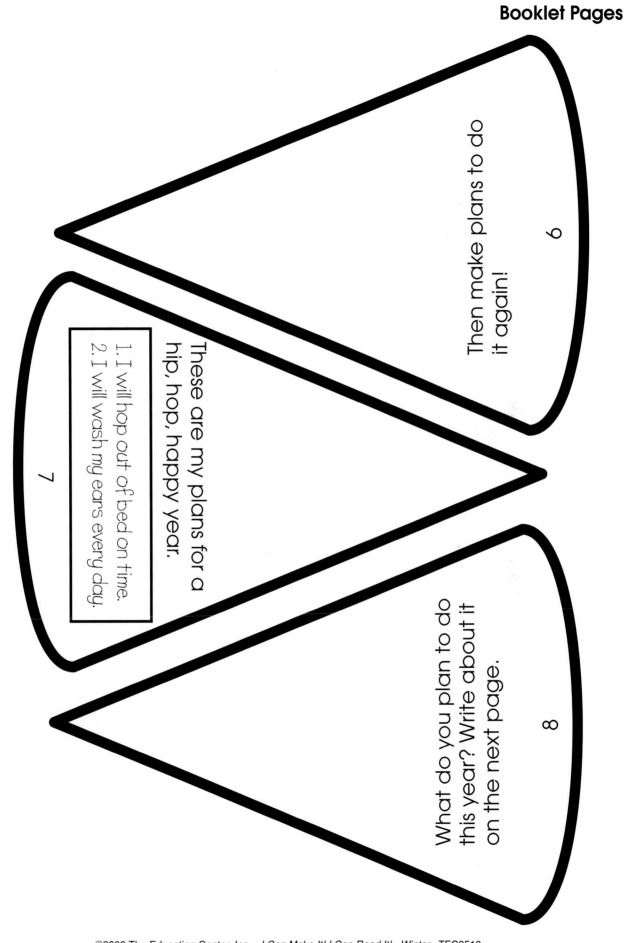

9

Then make plans to do it again!

7

These are my plans for a hip, hop, happy year.

1. I will hop out of bed on time.
2. I will wash my ears every day.

8

What do you plan to do this year? Write about it on the next page.

©2000 The Education Center, Inc. • *I Can Make It! I Can Read It!* • *Winter* • TEC3510

WINTER IS FUN!

Reading will be an icy blast with this snowflake booklet! Give each student a copy of pages 41–44. Have the student color and then cut out the snowflake and booklet pages. (Remind students to lightly color over the text so the story can be read.) Next, direct the student to stack her pages in numerical order, placing the cover on top. Have her center the pages on the snowflake and then staple them on the left-hand side. Then read a completed booklet with students. Provide time for students to read their booklets with one another. Encourage students to take their booklets home to read to family members. During these cold winter days, parents will love seeing how quickly reading skills are heating up!

CREATIVE DECORATING OPTIONS

- Using an old toothbrush, splatter watered-down blue and white tempera paint on the snowflake pattern.
- Use glitter glue to decorate the snowflake.

Extend this booklet activity and introduce youngsters to Old Man Winter by reading aloud *Is That You, Winter?* by Stephen Gammell (Harcourt Brace & Company, 1997).

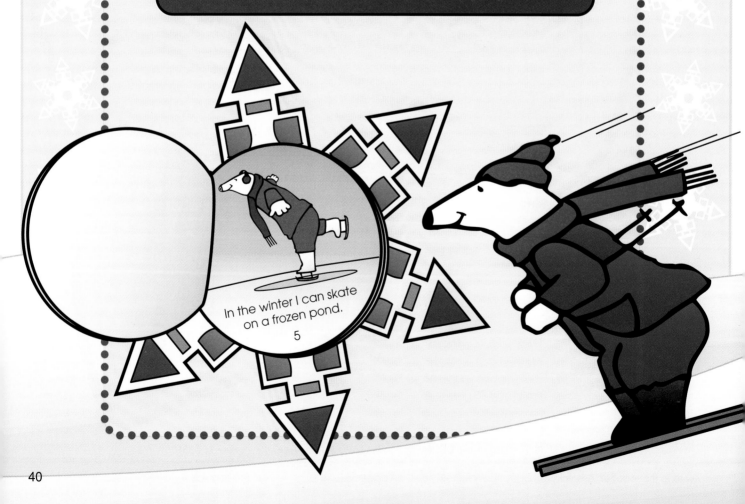

In the winter I can skate on a frozen pond.

5

Winter Is Fun!

_____
Name

©2000 The Education Center, Inc.

Winter is cold.
Winter is snowy.
Winter is icy.
Winter is fun!

1

In the winter I can build
a big snowman.

2

Note to the teacher: Use with "Winter Is Fun!" on page 40.

41

Booklet Pages

In the winter I can sled
down a snowy hill.
3

In the winter I can ski
down a mountain.
4

In the winter I can skate
on a frozen pond.
5

©2000 The Education Center, Inc. • *I Can Make It! I Can Read It!* • Winter • TEC3510

Note to the teacher: Use with "Winter Is Fun!" on page 40.

In the winter I can read
a book by the fire.
6

In the winter I can drink
hot chocolate.
7

Winter is cold.
Winter is snowy.
Winter is icy.
Winter is fun!
8

Note to the teacher: Use with "Winter Is Fun!" on page 40.

Booklet Pattern

Snowflake

Note to the teacher: Use with "Winter Is Fun!" on page 40.

A VERY COOL SHOW!

Watch youngsters warm up to winter *and* reading with this fashionable rhyming booklet! Give each student a copy of page 48 and white construction paper copies of pages 46 and 47. Have each student color and then cut out his booklet pages and patterns. (Remind the student to color lightly over the text so that the story can be read.) Next, direct him to stack his booklet pages in numerical order, placing the cover on top. Have him staple the stacked pages to his snowman bottom. Then instruct him to lightly glue the snowman top to the snowman bottom where indicated. When the glue has dried, read the completed booklet with students. Then provide time for each student to read his booklet with a buddy before sending it home to be read to family members. Snow *or* ice, reading this booklet is very nice!

CREATIVE DECORATING OPTIONS

- Glue colorful sequins on top of the snowman's buttons.
- Use glitter glue to decorate the snowman's scarf and hat.
- Using construction paper, add a bird to the snowman's hat.

Extend this booklet activity by reading aloud Lois Ehlert's wintry book *Snowballs* (Harcourt Brace & Company, 1995).

A Very Cool Show!

Ralph

Name

Booklet Pattern

Snowman Top

Note to the teacher: Use with "A Very Cool Show!" on page 45.

Snowman Bottom

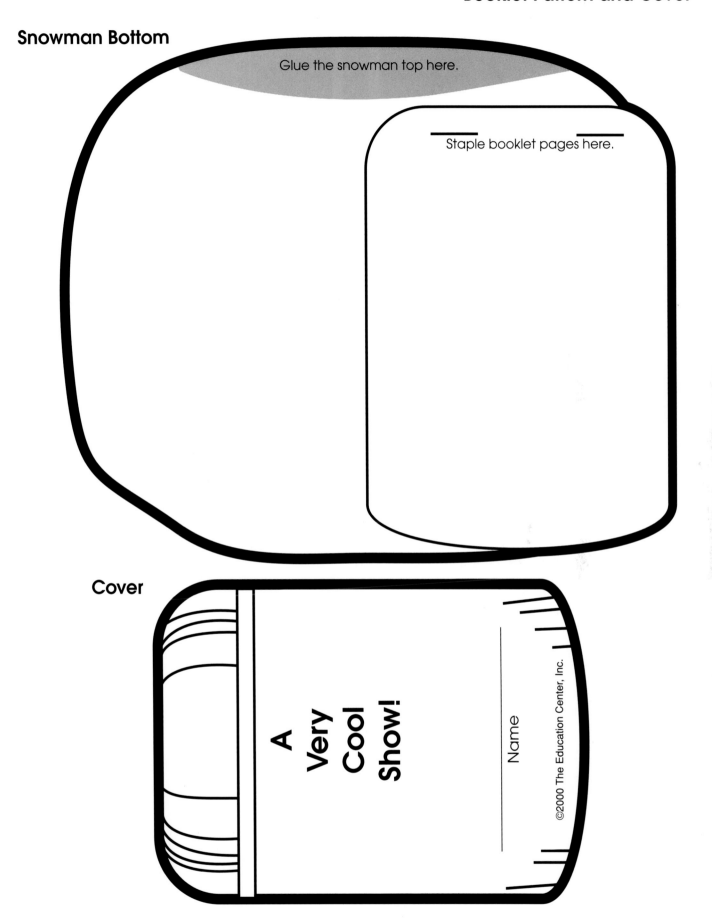

Glue the snowman top here.

Staple booklet pages here.

Cover

A
Very
Cool
Show!

Name

©2000 The Education Center, Inc.

Note to the teacher: Use with "A Very Cool Show!" on page 45.

47

Booklet Pages

When there is ice and snow,
I put on a fashion show!

1

When there is ice and snow,
Give me a top hat and bow.

2

When there is ice and snow,
I stand and wave hello.

3

But when there is rain or sun,
I am in trouble! Call 9-1-1!

4

WINTER IS FOR SLEEPING!

Take the chill out of winter with this informative animal booklet! Give each student a construction paper copy of page 52 and a copy of pages 50 and 51. Instruct the student to color and then cut out his booklet pattern, pages, and cover. Then direct him to fold his booklet pattern in half lengthwise and crease the fold. Then have him open the booklet pattern and cut on the dotted lines. Instruct him to glue each illustrated page to an inside flap. Have him glue the matching text beneath its picture. Next, direct the student to fold his booklet cover in half lengthwise and then glue the back of the booklet pattern to the inside as shown. Read a completed booklet with students. Provide time for each student to practice reading with a buddy. Then encourage the student to take his booklet home to read to family members. Parents will enjoy snuggling and reading on a cold winter day!

CREATIVE DECORATING OPTIONS

- To create a snowy scene, cut up doilies and glue the pieces to the cover.
- Using a Q-tip® cotton swab and white tempera paint, dot snowflakes on the cover.

Who sleeps through winter, when days are short and nights are long?

The bear sleeps tight in his warm den and waits for winter to be over. In the spring he will growl and eat fish again!

Extend this booklet activity by reading to students *Time to Sleep* by Denise Fleming (Henry Holt & Company, 1997).

Booklet Pattern

Who sleeps through winter, when days are short and nights are long?

Note to the teacher: Use with "Winter Is for Sleeping!" on page 49.

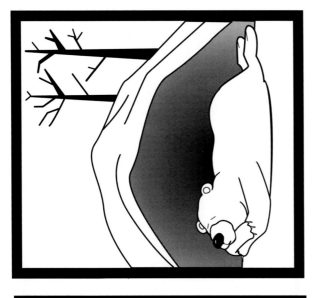

The bear sleeps tight in its warm den and waits for winter to be over. In the spring it will growl and eat fish again!

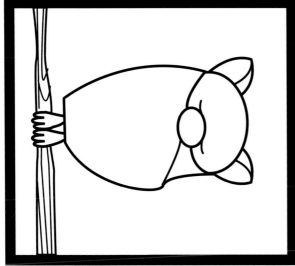

The bat hangs out and waits for winter to be over. In the spring it will fly and eat lots of bugs again!

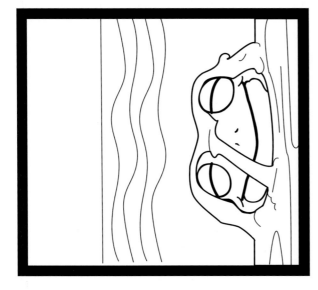

The frog digs into the mud and waits for winter to be over. In the spring it will jump and swim again!

Note to the teacher: Use with "Winter Is for Sleeping!" on page 49.

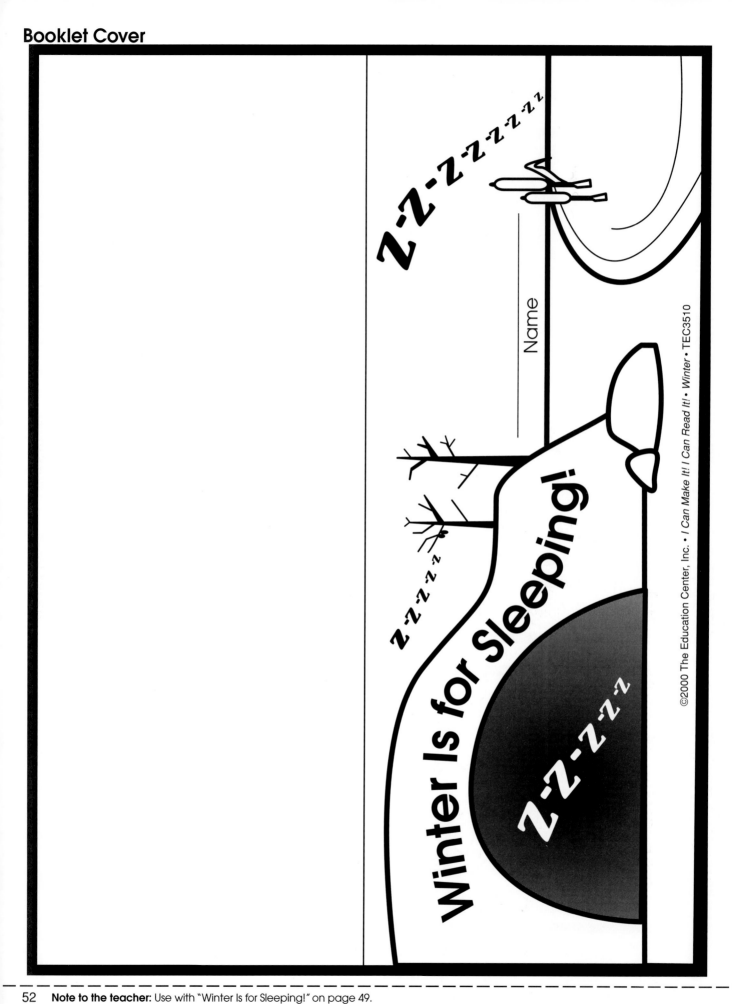

Name

Winter Is for Sleeping!

Z-Z-Z-Z-Z-Z-Z

z-z-z-z-z

Z-Z-Z-Z-Z

Booklet Cover

TAKE A WALK ON THE COLD SIDE!

Stroll through the bitterly cold polar regions in comfort with this informative polar animal booklet! Give each student a copy of pages 54–58. Have the student color and then cut out her booklet pages. (Remind students to color lightly over the text so the story can still be read.) Next, instruct her to stack her pages in numerical order, placing the cover on top. Staple the pages together on the left-hand side of the booklet. Then read a completed booklet with students. Provide time for each student to read her booklet with a buddy. Encourage her to take her booklet home to read to family members. Parents will agree—listening to their children read is a cool thing to do!

CREATIVE DECORATING OPTIONS

- Using scraps of wrapping paper or fabric, glue a hat and scarf on the cover polar bear.
- Glue scraps of aluminum foil on the cover's wintry background.

To extend this booklet activity, play Guess Who. Begin the game by saying, "I'm taking a walk on the cold side and I see an animal that…" Finish the statement with a fact about an animal described in the booklet. Encourage students to guess the answer. When a student correctly names the animal, have her read the fact from her booklet.

Way down south where it is very, very cold, the penguin goes for a walk.

The penguin has black and white feathers. He looks like he is going to a party, but he is going for a swim. He likes to dive from sea cliffs into the cold, cold water. He can't fly in the air, but when he swims, he looks like he is flying through the water.

Thanks for the walk on the cold side, penguin!

3

Booklet Cover

Take a Walk on the Cold Side!

Name

©2000 The Education Center, Inc. • *I Can Make It! I Can Read It!* • *Winter* • TEC3510

54   **Note to the teacher:** Use with "Take a Walk on the Cold Side!" on page 53.

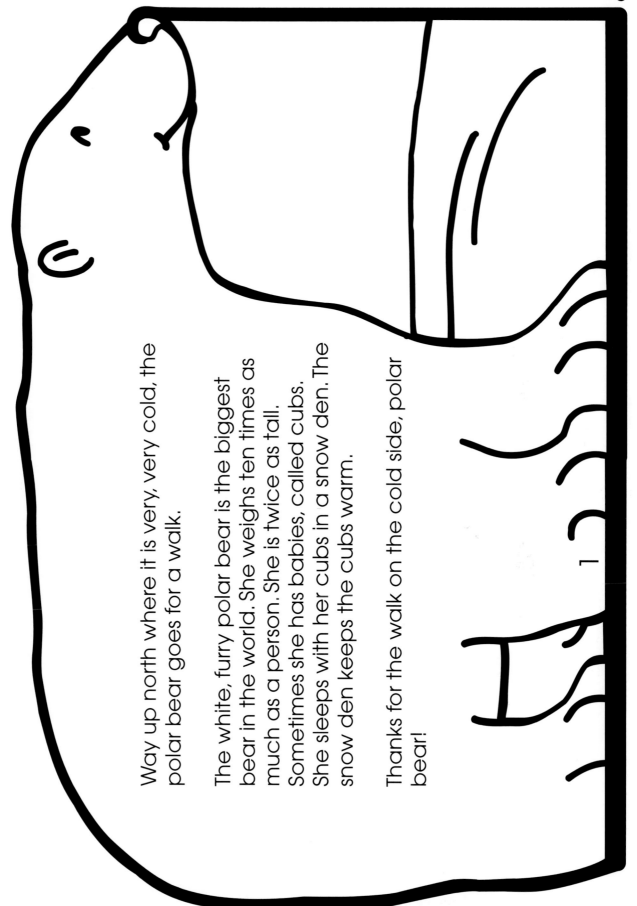

Way up north where it is very, very, very cold, the polar bear goes for a walk.

The white, furry polar bear is the biggest bear in the world. She weighs ten times as much as a person. She is twice as tall. Sometimes she has babies, called cubs. She sleeps with her cubs in a snow den. The snow den keeps the cubs warm.

Thanks for the walk on the cold side, polar bear!

1

Note to the teacher: Use with "Take a Walk on the Cold Side!" on page 53.

Booklet Page

Way up north, where it is very, very, very cold, the wolf goes for a walk.

The wolf is part of the dog family. He can see, hear, and smell very well. That makes him a great hunter. When the wolf and his friends go hunting, they greet each other with a howl. Their howling tells other wolves to stay away.

Thanks for the walk on the cold side, wolf!

2

Note to the teacher: Use with "Take a Walk on the Cold Side!" on page 53.

Way down south where it is very, very cold, the penguin goes for a walk.

The penguin has black and white feathers. He looks like he is going to a party, but he is going for a swim. He likes to dive from sea cliffs into the cold, cold water. He can't fly in the air, but when he swims, he looks like he is flying through the water.

Thanks for the walk on the cold side, penguin!

3

Note to the teacher: Use with "Take a Walk on the Cold Side!" on page 53.

Booklet Page

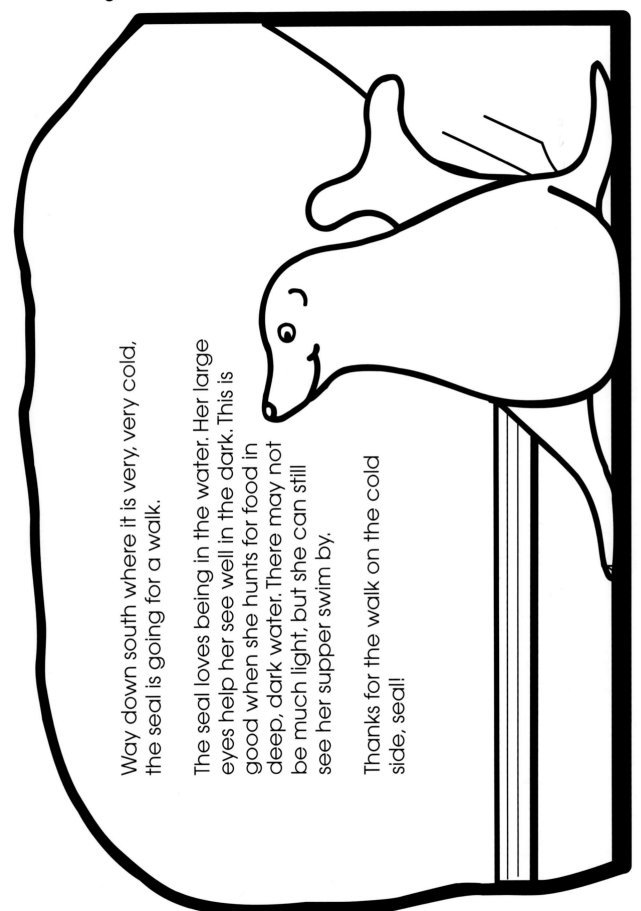

Way down south where it is very, very cold, the seal is going for a walk.

The seal loves being in the water. Her large eyes help her see well in the dark. This is good when she hunts for food in deep, dark water. There may not be much light, but she can still see her supper swim by.

Thanks for the walk on the cold side, seal!

Note to the teacher: Use with "Take a Walk on the Cold Side!" on page 53.

TEN LITTLE PENGUINS

Melt away those winter humdrums with this interactive penguin booklet! Give each student a copy of pages 60–64. Instruct the student to color her cover, penguin cards, pocket, and ice caps. Then have her cut out the booklet cover, patterns, and pages on the bold lines. Next, direct her to apply glue to the gray area of the cover. Then have her align and press the pocket on top of the glue. Instruct her to stack her booklet pages in numerical order and staple them to the ice caps where indicated. Next, have her staple the cover to the ice caps where indicated. To read the booklet, have her place it flat upon her desk. Then invite her to randomly arrange her ten penguin cards on the ice caps. As each page is read, direct her to take off one of the cards and set it aside. When she is finished reading the booklet, she stores the ten penguin cards in the cover pocket. Provide time for her to practice reading her booklet with a buddy. Then send the booklet home for her to read to family members.

CREATIVE DECORATING OPTIONS

- On the cover, apply glue to the background and press salt onto it to create a polar landscape.
- Use watercolors to paint the ocean.

Read the rollicking tale *Tacky the Penguin* by Helen Lester (Houghton Mifflin Company, 1990) to extend this booklet activity.

Six little penguins went for a dive.
One swam away and then there were five.

5

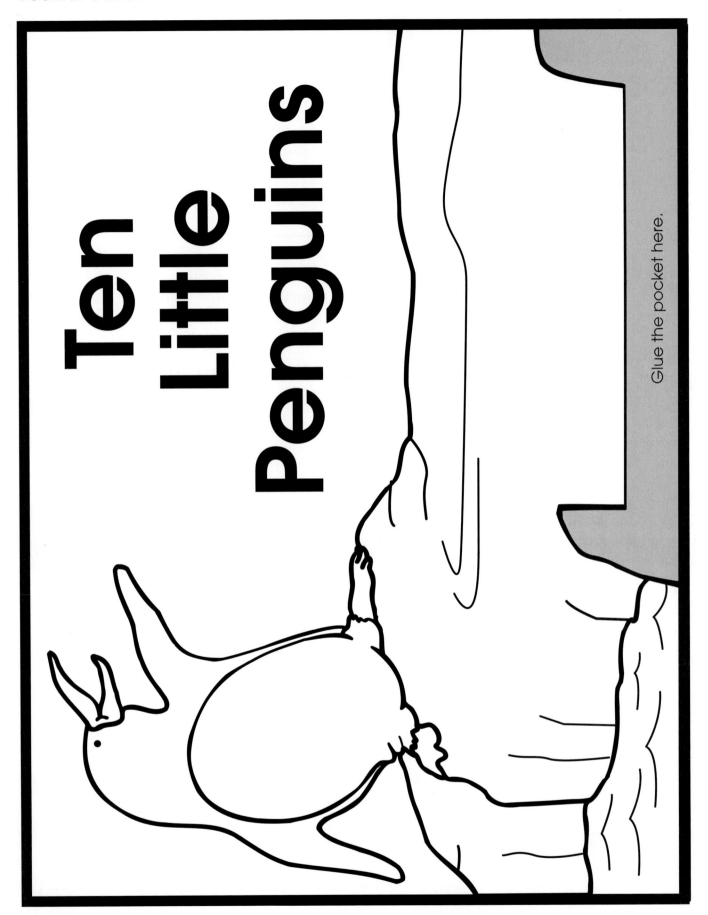

Ten Little Penguins

Glue the pocket here.

Ten little penguins walked in a line.
One stopped to play and then there were nine.

1

Nine little penguins went for a skate.
One fell down and then there were eight.

2

Eight little penguins counted to ten.
One went to hide and then there were seven.

3

Seven little penguins watched the chicks.
One found an egg and then there were six.

4

Six little penguins went for a dive.
One swam away and then there were five.

5

Five little penguins played on the shore.
One saw a seal and then there were four.

6

Four little penguins swam in the sea.
One chased a fish and then there were three.

7

Three little penguins with nothing to do.
One went home and then there were two.

8

Two little penguins were having fun.
One got tired and then there was one.

9

One little penguin missed his brothers
He went off to find the others.

10

Booklet Page

No little penguins were waddling around.
The ten little penguins could not be found!

11

Penguin Cards

Pocket

_____
Name

- -

Note to the teacher: Use with "Ten Little Penguins" on page 59.

Booklet Pattern
Ice Caps

Staple the booklet pages here.

Staple the booklet cover here.

Note to the teacher: Use with "Ten Little Penguins" on page 59.

TELL ME ABOUT THE PRESIDENT!

Salute the office of the American president with this informative booklet! Give each student a copy of pages 66–71 and a 6" x 9" piece of red, white, or blue construction paper. Have the student color and then cut out the cover patterns and booklet pages. Next, have her stack her pages in numerical order. Direct her to place the stacked pages in the center of the piece of construction paper (see the illustration) and staple them at the top. Then instruct her to align Cover B on the left-hand side of the booklet so that the stars are in the upper left-hand corner. Staple Cover B to the construction paper along the left-hand side, making sure not to staple through the booklet pages. Staple Cover A to the right-hand side of the construction paper as shown. Then read a completed booklet with students, assisting them with filling in the answers on booklet page 9. Provide time for students to read their booklets with one another. Encourage students to take their booklets home to read to family members.

CREATIVE DECORATING OPTIONS

- Glue a newspaper or magazine picture of the current president and first lady to the cover.
- Using red liquid tempera paint, press thumbprints along the rows to make red stripes.

Extend this booklet activity by having each student write what she would do as president of the United States. Invite her to read her response to the class and then staple it in her booklet.

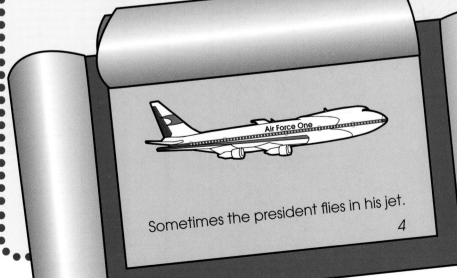

Sometimes the president flies in his jet.

4

Tell Me About the President!

©2000 The Education Center, Inc. • *I Can Make It! I Can Read It!* • *Winter* • TEC3510

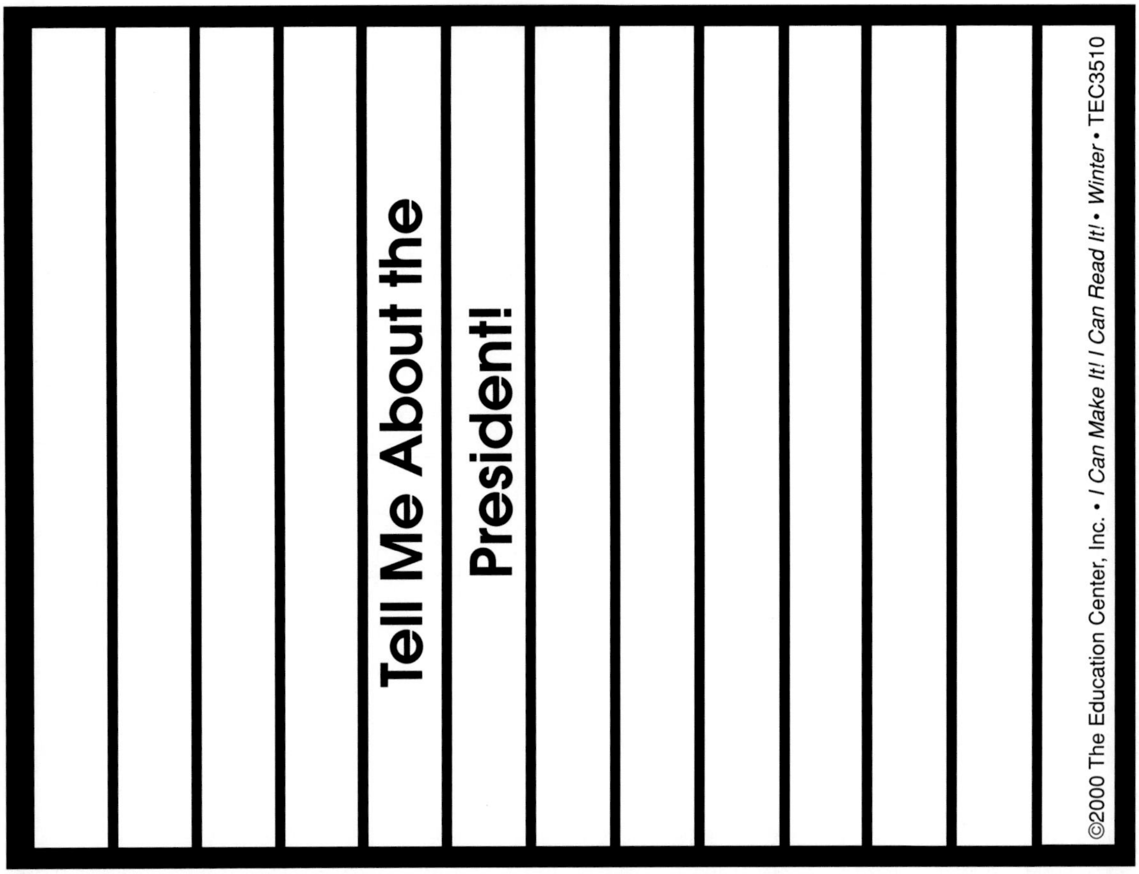

Cover B

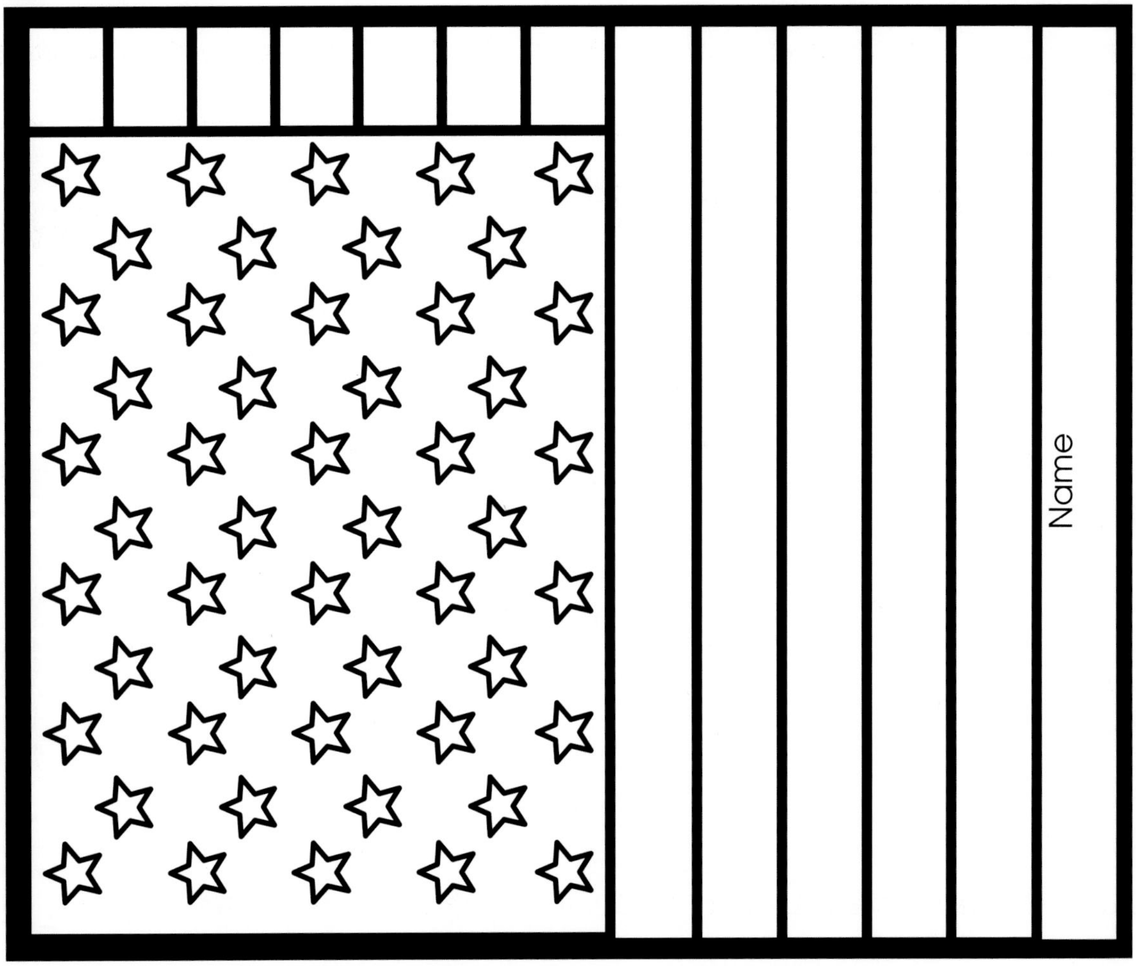

Name

Note to the teacher: Use with "Tell Me About the President!" on page 65.

The leader of the United States of America is the president.

1

The president lives and works in the White House. The White House has 132 rooms.

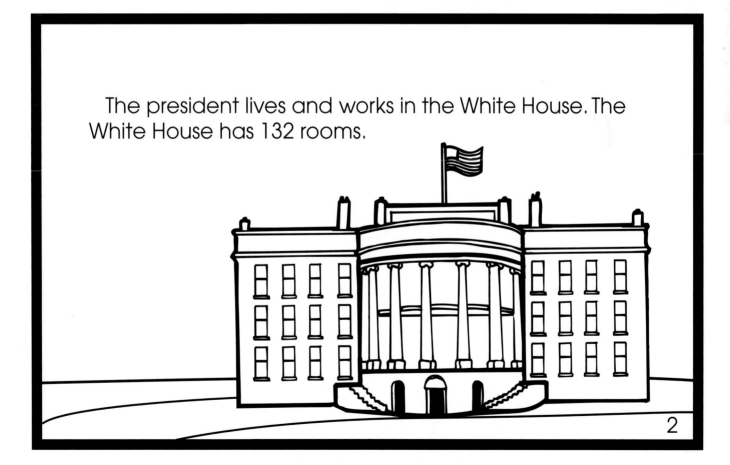

2

The president does many jobs. He helps make the laws. He meets with the leaders of other countries.

3

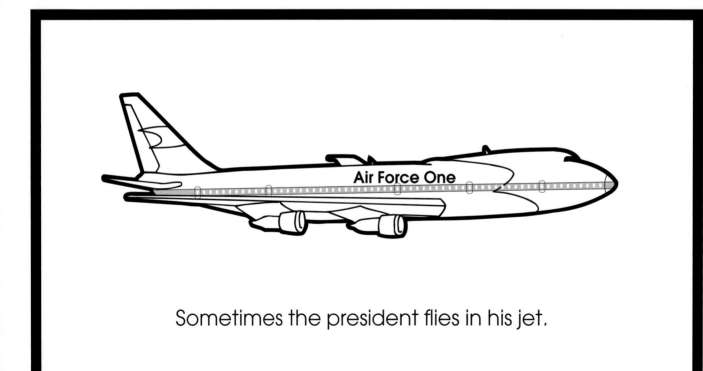

Sometimes the president flies in his jet.

4

©2000 The Education Center, Inc. • *I Can Make It! I Can Read It!* • Winter • TEC3510

The wife of the president is called the first lady. The first lady helps the president with his job.

Martha Washington

5

The president has people to keep him safe. They make sure the president's food is safe to eat. They make sure the president is safe at all times.

6

Note to the teacher: Use with "Tell Me About the President!" on page 65.

George Washington and Abraham Lincoln are two presidents that everyone knows.

7

Some presidents can be seen on money.

8

Who is the president of the United States?

_____

– –

_____

Who is the first lady of the United States?

_____

– –

_____

9

The president works for us every day. He works hard for the people.

10

BLACK AMERICAN STARS

Salute four dynamic Black Americans with this informative booklet! Give each student a copy of pages 74 and 75 and a construction paper copy of page 73. Have the student color the booklet patterns and then cut out the booklet backing and patterns. For each pattern, have him fold forward the edge with the dotted line. Starting with Oprah Winfrey and finishing with Sherian Cadoria, have the student glue each star's folded edge to the backing where indicated. Let the glue dry. Then read a completed booklet with students, starting with the text behind Sherian Cadoria and finishing with Oprah Winfrey. Provide time for students to practice reading their booklets with one another. Encourage students to take their booklets home to read to family members. Your young readers will shine with this reading activity!

CREATIVE DECORATING OPTIONS

- Glue the booklet to the center of a 9" x 12" sheet of blue construction paper. Then, using liquid tempera paint and a star-shaped sponge, print a design around the border.
- Add star stickers to the finished booklet.

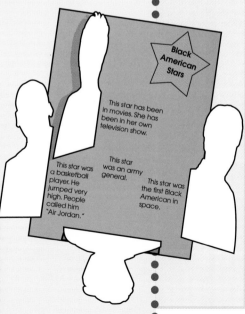

Extend this booklet activity by having a class discussion about famous Black Americans, such as Jackie Robinson and Harriet Tubman. List the names on the chalkboard. Next, have each student write and illustrate a sentence about one of the people listed. Then staple it to the back of his booklet.

Black
American
Stars

Glue Oprah Winfrey's flap here.

This star has been
in movies. She has
been in her own
television show.

Glue Michael Jordan's flap here.

This star
was an army
general.

Glue Guy Bluford's flap here.

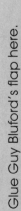

This star was
a basketball
player. He
jumped very
high. People
called him
"Air Jordan."

This star was
the first Black
American in
space.

Glue Sherian Cadoria's flap here.

Note to the teacher: Use with "Black American Stars" on page 72.

Booklet Patterns

Michael
Jordan

Sherian
Cadoria

©2000 The Education Center, Inc.

Note to the teacher: Use with "Black American Stars" on page 72.

Oprah
Winfrey

Guy
Bluford

Note to the teacher: Use with "Black American Stars" on page 72.

IS IT TO BE WINTER? IS IT TO BE SPRING?

It's predicted beyond a shadow of a doubt! Students will go hog-wild over these pop-up booklets! Give each student a copy of pages 77–79 and two sheets of 9" x 12" construction paper. Have the student cut out the cover illustrations, pop-ups, and booklet pages on the bold outer lines. Instruct her to fold each booklet page in half so the dotted lines are showing. Then have her cut on the dotted lines. Help her to fold the resulting strip as shown. Next, direct her to fold in half both sheets of construction paper. Instruct the student to center a booklet page on one sheet of construction paper so that the creases are aligned. Then have her glue the edges of the booklet page to the construction paper. Direct her to glue the remaining booklet page to the second sheet of construction paper in the same manner. Next, instruct the student to glue the corresponding pop-up to the booklet pages as shown. Then have her fold each booklet in half, glue the appropriate cover to the front, and personalize it. When the glue is dry, invite the student to color her pages to illustrate the season. Next, align the backs of her two completed booklets and staple them together. Demonstrate how to read the two booklets by reading one and then flipping the booklet over to read the other. Provide time for each student to read her booklet with a buddy before sending it home to be read to family members. Good readers will be popping up all over the place!

CREATIVE DECORATING OPTION

- On the winter cover, glue cotton to represent snow. On the spring cover, glue construction paper flowers.

Extend this booklet activity by reading aloud Bruce Koscielniak's entertaining book *Geoffrey Groundhog Predicts the Weather* (Houghton Mifflin Company, 1995).

Hello! I am Mr. Groundhog! On February 2, I will get up from a long winter nap. I will leave my den. If the sun is shining and I see my shadow, I will jump back into my den. There will be six more weeks of winter.

Is It to Be Spring?

Is It to Be Winter?

Cover Illustrations

Is It to Be Winter?

Is It to Be Spring?

Spring Pop-Up

Winter Pop-Up

Note to the teacher: Use with "Is It to Be Winter? Is It to Be Spring?" on page 76.

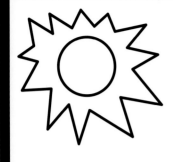

Hello! I am Mr. Groundhog! On February 2, I will get up from a long winter nap. I will leave my den. If the sun is shining and I see my shadow, I will jump back into my den. There will be six more weeks of winter.

Note to the teacher: Use with "Is It to Be Winter? Is It to Be Spring?" on page 76.

Hello! I am Mr. Groundhog! On February 2, I will get up from a long winter nap. I will leave my den. If it is cloudy outside and I don't see my shadow, then spring will come soon!

BE MINE!

Treat students to this sweet rhyming valentine booklet and boost their reading confidence! Give each student a copy of pages 81–82 and a 14-inch length of narrow ribbon or yarn. Have students color the envelope and booklet pages. (Remind each student to color lightly over the text so the booklet can be read.) Then instruct him to cut out the envelope and pages on the bold lines. To assemble the booklet, direct him to stack the pages in numerical order, punch holes where indicated, and tie the pages together with ribbon or yarn as illustrated. To make the envelope, instruct him to fold back Flaps 1 and 2 on the dotted lines. Next, have him apply glue to the gray areas and then fold back Flap 3. Direct him to press Flap 3 to the glued areas. Then read a completed booklet with students. Demonstrate how to place the booklet in the envelope and fold down Flap 4. Provide time for each student to read with a buddy before taking his completed booklet home to read to family members. Reading this booklet to loved ones comes straight from the heart!

CREATIVE DECORATING OPTIONS

- Add heart stickers to the booklet pages and envelope.
- Using fabric scraps, cut out heart shapes and glue them to the envelope.

Dear Valentine,
I like you when you are happy.
I like you when you are sad.
I like you when you are good.
I like you when you are bad.

1

Be Mine!

To extend this booklet activity, invite students to write their own valentine verses and add them to the envelope.

I like you every day.
I like you every night.
I like you when it is dark.
I like you when it is light.

2

So, won't you be my valentine
On this special day?
Lots of hearts and candy
Are coming your way!

Your Valentine,
_____

4

Dear Valentine,
I like you when you are happy.
I like you when you are sad.
I like you when you are good.
I like you when you are bad.

1

I like you when you smile.
I like you when you frown.
I like you when you are up.
I like you when you are down.

3

Note to the teacher: Use with "Be Mine!" on page 80.

Booklet Pattern

Envelope

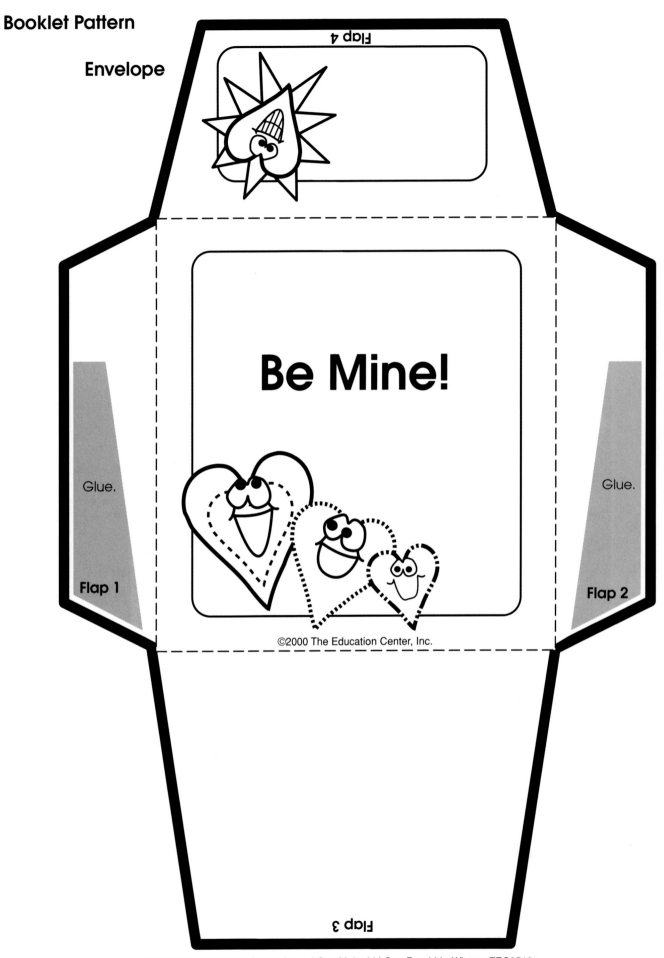

Flap 4

Glue.

Flap 1

Be Mine!

Glue.

Flap 2

©2000 The Education Center, Inc.

Flap 3

MAY WE MAKE A DEAL?

Add a touch of magic to your reading program with this tooth fairy tale! Give each student a copy of pages 84–87. Instruct the student to color the illustration on page 87. Then have him cut out the cover and booklet pages on the bold outer lines. Next, direct him to stack his pages in numerical order, placing the cover on top. Have him align the stacked pages with the tooth on booklet page 6. Staple the pages along the left-hand side. Then read a completed booklet with students. Provide time for students to read their booklets with one another. Encourage students to take their booklets home to read to family members. Reading the tooth truth to friends and family members will promote big smiles!

CREATIVE DECORATING OPTIONS

- Apply glitter glue along the dotted lines of the illustration.
- Apply small star stickers to the fairy's robe.

Extend this booklet activity by having each youngster count the number of teeth in his mouth. Calculate the total and post it on a wall chart. Then each time a student loses a tooth, change the total.

May We Make a Deal?

Richard

Name

Booklet Cover and Page

Cover

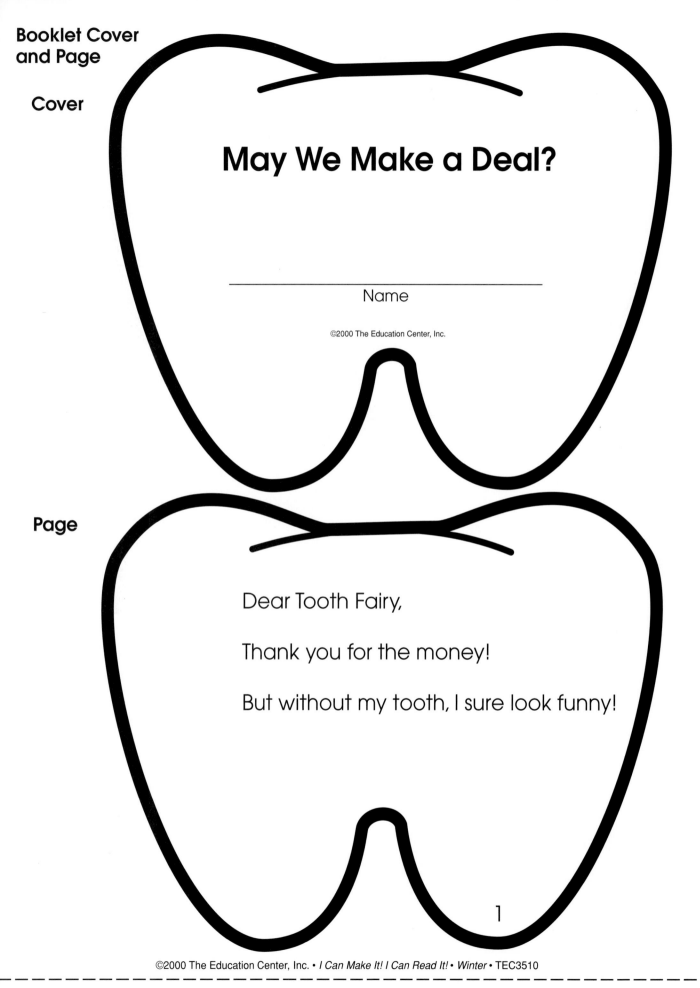

May We Make a Deal?

_____
Name

©2000 The Education Center, Inc.

Page

Dear Tooth Fairy,

Thank you for the money!

But without my tooth, I sure look funny!

1

Note to the teacher: Use with "May We Make a Deal?" on page 83.

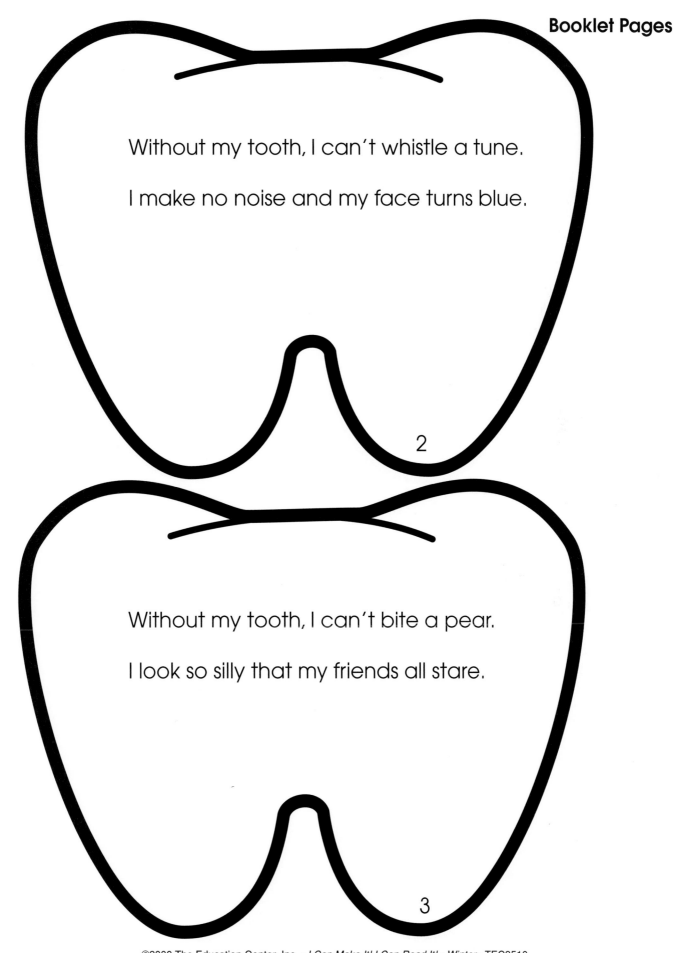

Without my tooth, I can't whistle a tune.

I make no noise and my face turns blue.

2

Without my tooth, I can't bite a pear.

I look so silly that my friends all stare.

3

©2000 The Education Center, Inc. • *I Can Make It! I Can Read It!* • *Winter* • TEC3510

Without my tooth, I can't drink through a straw.

I make the biggest mess you ever saw.

4

Without my tooth, nothing is going well.

I miss my tooth as you can tell.

5

So I'd like to make a deal and that's the truth.

Please take your money and leave my tooth!

6

Note to the teacher: Use with "May We Make a Deal?" on page 83.

LUCKY'S GOLD

Send your young readers in search of the gold with this interactive St. Patrick's Day booklet! Give each student a copy of pages 90–91 and a green construction paper copy of page 89. Have the student color her booklet patterns on page 91 and then cut out her booklet pages and patterns (pages 89–91). Direct her to stack her booklet pages in numerical order and staple them to the backing. Then instruct her to glue the head to the backing where indicated. Have her fold the jacket on the dotted lines as shown. Instruct her to glue the pocket to the pants where indicated and the sleeves to the back of the jacket as illustrated. Next, have her glue the hands to the jacket sleeves and the top hat to the gray area of the bottom hat. Finally, have her glue each top shoe to a bottom shoe where indicated and then glue the shoes to the pant legs. When the glue has dried, read a completed booklet with students. Demonstrate how to lift each flap and unfold the hands to find the hidden gold. Then provide time for students to practice reading their booklets with one another. Encourage students to take their booklets home to read to family members.

CREATIVE DECORATING OPTIONS

- Apply gold glitter glue or gold circular seals to the coins.
- Glue a button to the jacket.

Extend this booklet activity by reading aloud *The Last Snake in Ireland* by Sheila MacGill Callahan (Holiday House, Inc; 2000).

Jacket and Pants Backing

Booklet Patterns

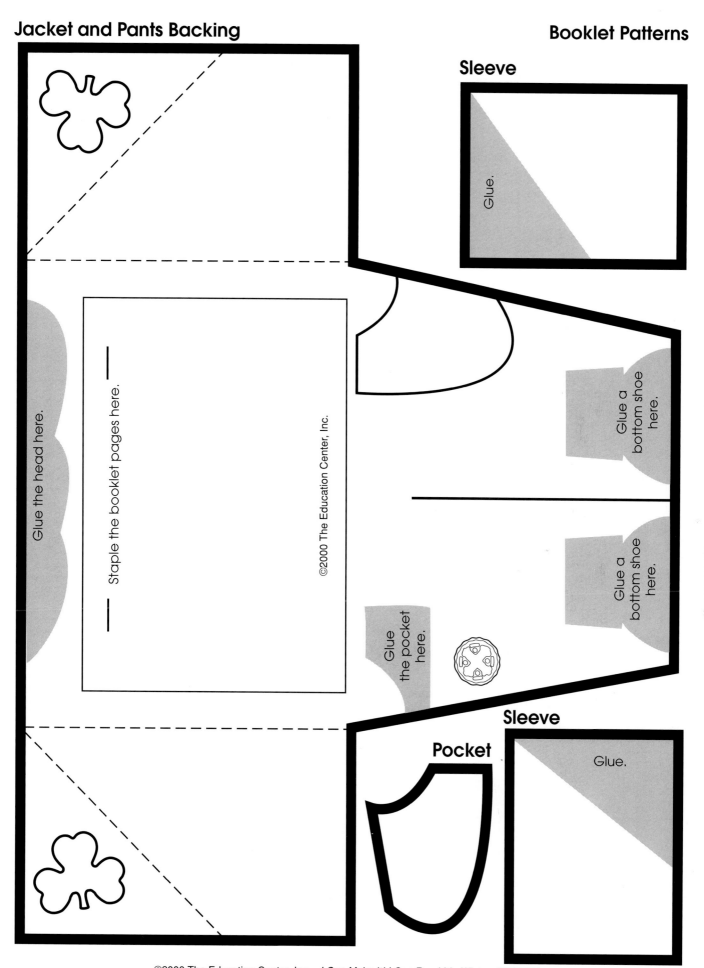

Sleeve

Glue.

Glue a bottom shoe here.

Glue a bottom shoe here.

Glue the head here.

Staple the booklet pages here.

©2000 The Education Center, Inc.

Glue the pocket here.

Sleeve

Glue.

Pocket

Note to the teacher: Use with "Lucky's Gold" on page 88.

Booklet Pages

He hides gold in a pocket.
He hides gold in his hands.

2

I can find Lucky's gold, can you?

4

Lucky's Gold

Lucky likes to hide his gold.
He thinks no one can find it.

1

He hides gold in his hat.
He hides gold in his shoes.

3

Note to the teacher: Use with "Lucky's Gold" on page 88.

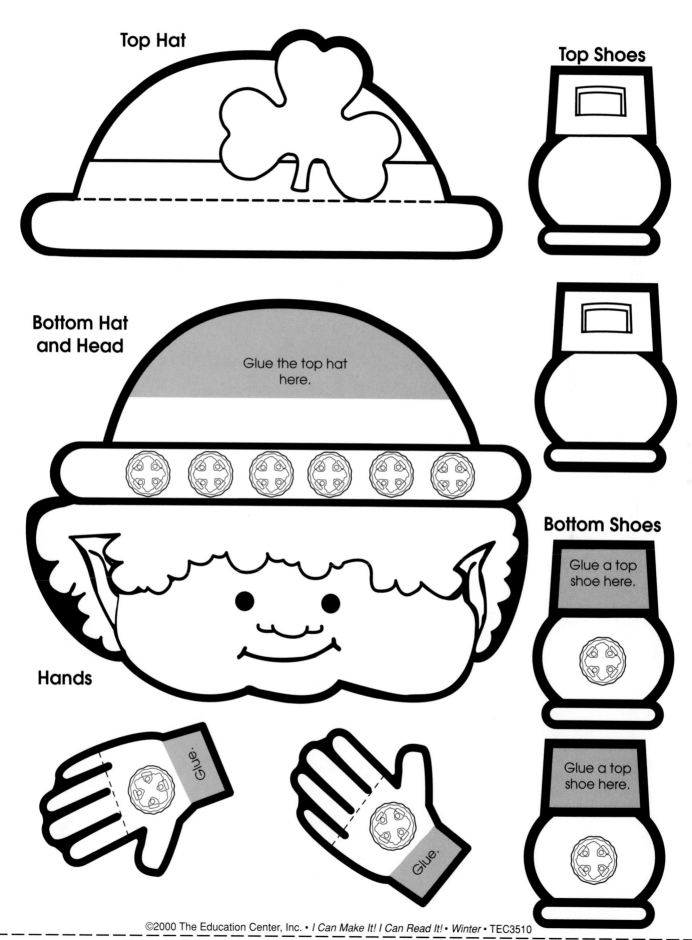

Top Hat

Top Shoes

Bottom Hat and Head

Glue the top hat here.

Hands

Bottom Shoes

Glue a top shoe here.

Glue a top shoe here.

Glue.

Glue.

©2000 The Education Center, Inc. • *I Can Make It! I Can Read It!* • Winter • TEC3510

Note to the teacher: Use with "Lucky's Gold" on page 88.

91

GETTING TO KNOW DINOSAURS

Here's one big booklet that will have enormous appeal with your young readers! Give each student a copy of pages 93–96. Have the student color her booklet pages and then cut them out along the bold outer lines. Next, instruct her to sequence the cut-outs and lay them end to end. Direct her to glue the booklet pages together where indicated to create one long strip (caution students to keep the cutouts in the proper order). Using the lines as guides, help her accordion-fold the pages as shown. Then read a booklet with students. Provide time for each student to practice reading with a partner. Encourage students to take their completed booklets home to read to family members. Reading is "dino-mite"!

CREATIVE DECORATING OPTIONS

- Dab colored glue on the dinosaur to create scales.
- Using a Q-tip® cotton swab and liquid tempera paint, print a colorful texture on the plates and spikes along the dinosaur's back.

Getting to Know
Dinosaurs

Sarah
Name

Big dinosaurs were the largest animals to ever live on land.

Some dinosaurs were very tall. They were taller than a house.

Some dinosaurs were very small. They were as small as a chicken.

Some dinosaurs could run very fast.

Others were very slow.
Some dinosaurs could fly.

Big or small, fast or slow,
Dinosaurs lived a long time ago.

Extend this booklet activity by reading to students the rollicking story *Dinorella: A Prehistoric Fairy Tale* by Pamela Duncan Edwards (Hyperion Books for Children, 1997).

Getting to Know
Dinosaurs

_____
Name

Note to the teacher: Use with "Getting to Know Dinosaurs" on page 92.

93

Big dinosaurs were the largest animals to ever live on land.

Some dinosaurs were very tall. They were taller than a house.

Some dinosaurs were very small. They were as small as a chicken.

Glue here.

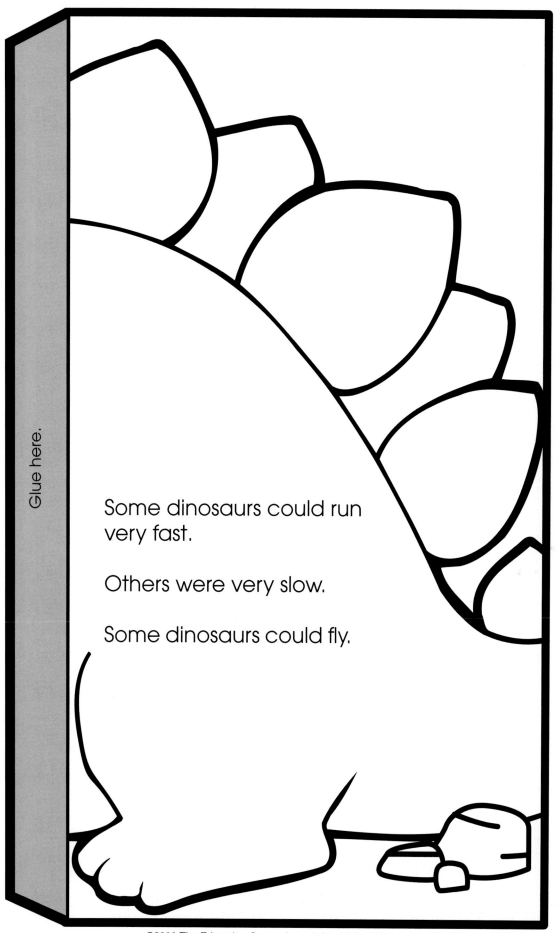

Glue here.

Some dinosaurs could run very fast.

Others were very slow.

Some dinosaurs could fly.

Note to the teacher: Use with "Getting to Know Dinosaurs" on page 92.

Booklet Page

Glue here.

Big or small, fast or slow,
Dinosaurs lived a long time ago.